DATE DUE

NO 10 '94			
AP 29 '95			
OC 15 '96			
AP 16 '97			
JAN 26 '98			
261-2500		Printed in USA

For her aid to the poor of India, Mother Teresa was
awarded the Nobel Peace Prize in 1979.

MOTHER TERESA

Friend of the Friendless

By Carol Greene

 CHILDRENS PRESS, CHICAGO

For Rachel Drennen

Photos Credits

Wide World Photos—Cover, 2, 14, 15

United Press International Photo—12, 17, 19, 21, 22 (2 photos), 23, 24, 25, 26 (3 photos), 28, 29 (2 photos), 30 (3 photos)

Len Meents—6, 8, 10

Library of Congress Cataloging in Publication Data

Greene, Carol.
  Mother Teresa: friend of the friendless.

  (Easy-to-read biographies)
  Summary: Describes the work of Mother Teresa with the poor of India and how she came to devote her life to bringing not just goods and services to those in need, but also love.
    1. Teresa, Mother, 1910-   —Juvenile literature.
  2. Nuns—India—Calcutta—Biography—Juvenile literature.
  3. Calcutta (India)—Biography—Juvenile literature.
  [1. Teresa, Mother, 1910-   2. Nuns] I. Title.
  II. Series.
  BX4406.5.Z8G73   1983   271ʹ.97   [B] [92]   83-7386
  ISBN 0-516-03559-2

MOTHER TERESA
Friend of the Friendless

Her Own Road

Agnes was an ordinary little girl. She loved her family. She loved music. She loved trips to the mountains.

Agnes was born on August 27, 1910. Her full name was Agnes Gonxha Bojaxhiu. She had an older brother and an older sister. Her family was from Albania. But they lived in Skopje (SKOHP-yeh), Yugoslavia.

Agnes went to a public school in Skopje. She went to a Roman Catholic church. She was a happy, ordinary little girl.

Mother Teresa as a teenager

Then one day when Agnes was
twelve, something happened.
That something changed her
whole life. She wouldn't be
ordinary anymore.

Agnes met a Catholic priest
who worked in India. He talked
about that strange, beautiful

country. He talked about his missionary work. He said that each person must follow his or her own road in life.

"Why, I must follow my own road, too!" thought Agnes. "I wonder what that road will be. Should *I* be a missionary?"

She talked to the priest. He told her to wait. "God will tell you what you must do," he said.

Agnes waited for six years. Then the priest came for another visit.

"I know what I must do now," Agnes told him. "I must be a missionary — maybe to India."

Mother Teresa at the convent of the Sisters of Loreto in Ireland.

The priest told her about a religious order in Ireland called the Sisters of Our Lady of Loreto. They did missionary work in India.

10

So Agnes left her home and went to Ireland. She studied with the nuns for a year. Then they sent her to her new home — India.

Women usually change their names when they become nuns. Each takes the name of a saint she admires. Agnes chose the name Teresa.

At first Sister Teresa taught in a high school in Calcutta, India. She loved teaching and she did a good job. Before long she became principal of the school.

In India, Mother Teresa, holding one of the children from an
orphanage, is known as the "saint of the slums."

One night, Sister Teresa was traveling on a train in India. All at once she began to see pictures. But she didn't see them with her eyes. She was not seeing the people and things around her. With her mind and her heart, Sister Teresa saw the poor people who lived in Calcutta.

These people suffered terribly. Many were sick. They had no money, no homes, no food. Worst of all, they had no one to love them.

"These are the people God wants me to serve," said Sister Teresa to herself.

In 1948 she left the other nuns
in Calcutta. She went to another
city and studied health care. She
knew she would need new skills
to help the poor.

Then, on Christmas Eve, Sister
Teresa came back to Calcutta.
She had no home now. She had
almost no money. She was all
alone. But she knew what she
must do.

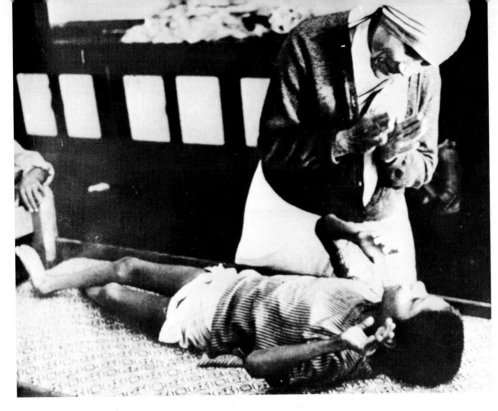

Mother Teresa comforts a sick child.

Sister Teresa found five children who lived in the streets. No one else wanted them. So she took them to a park and began to teach them.

By Christmas Day she had twenty-five unwanted children. By New Year's Day she had forty-one. Sister Teresa was not alone anymore. And the children had someone to love them.

Sister Teresa lived like the poor people. That way she felt close to them and they felt close to her. Soon she moved into a room in an attic. An Indian man had given it to her.

Sister Teresa did not think others would want to live that way. But she was wrong. One day a young Indian woman came to see her. Sister Teresa had taught her in the high school.

"I want to work with you," said the young woman.

Soon nine other young women said the same thing. All of them had been Sister Teresa's students. Now they were her new family of nuns and she was Mother Teresa.

The Missionaries of Charity wear blue-lined white cotton saris.

Mother Teresa called her nuns the Missionaries of Charity. Each promised to love and serve poor people. Each wore a simple robe called a *sari*. These saris were cheap ones like those worn by poor Indian women. But to the people the nuns served, they were beautiful.

Angels in the Slums

One day Mother Teresa was walking along a street in the Calcutta slums. Suddenly she saw a woman lying on a pile of rubbish. She was dying. It was terrible.

Mother Teresa picked up the woman. She carried her to a hospital. The hospital workers didn't want to take the dying woman. But Mother Teresa said she wouldn't leave until they did. She won.

Soon after that, city officials gave Mother Teresa a building to use for terribly sick people. She called it *Nirmal Hriday.* That means "Pure Heart."

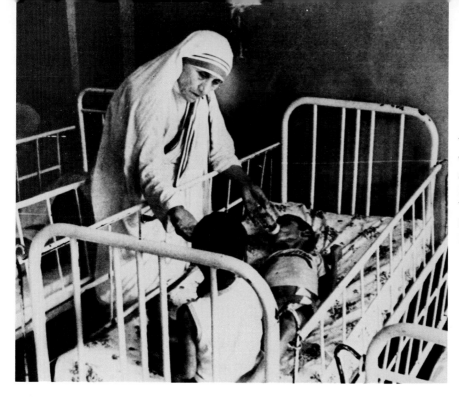

Today her missionary work takes place all over the world. Here we see Mother Teresa feeding a hungry child in East Beirut, Lebanon.

Mother Teresa and her nuns fed and cared for the people at Pure Heart. Some of them were too sick to get well. They died. But at least they died in a clean place cared for by people who loved them. And some people did get well.

More and more people began giving Mother Teresa money for her work. The Indian government helped her, too.

Mother Teresa used the money to buy things for the poor. She started schools and hospitals. She set up kitchens where the poor could get a meal. She set up places where they could get free medicine. She opened orphanages for unwanted children. And she helped many of these children find homes and families to love them.

In 1964, Pope Paul VI visited India. Some Americans gave him a new white Lincoln convertible to use while he was there. When he left, he gave the car to Mother Teresa.

She never even rode in it. Instead, she sold it. Then she used the money to start a village for people with leprosy. (Leprosy

Pope Paul VI presented Mother Teresa with a statue of the Madonna when he awarded her the Pope John XXIII Peace Prize in 1971.

is a disease. It attacks the skin and nerves. If it is not treated, lepers get lumps on their skin and lose feeling in their face, arms, and legs. It can lead to physical deformities. More than ten million people in the world have leprosy. Most of them live in warm climates.)

Mother Teresa has been welcomed by
President and Mrs. Reagan (left)
and by Pope John Paul II (above).

As time went by, many women
—and men, too—came to work
with Mother Teresa. Soon there
were Missionaries of Charity all
over India.

Some went to other countries,
such as Italy, England, Tanzania,
El Salvador, and the United
States. Wherever they went they
found plenty of poor people to
help.

Mother Teresa (left) and her fellow workers kneel in prayer at their headquarters in Calcutta, India. Her sisters work with the poorest people in India and in 30 other countries.

Mother Teresa and her workers are busy. They get up early. They do their chores, say their prayers, and have a church service. Then they go to work.

Some work in the schools, kitchens, or other places where poor people come. Some go out in the streets and look for people who need help. Some visit sick people. Some visit old people that no one else cares about.

23

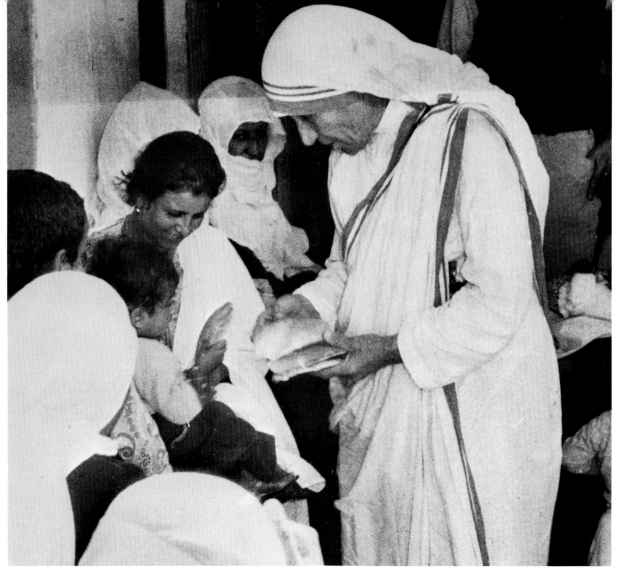

Mother Teresa says, "Love one another as God loves each one of you."

Mother Teresa believes that the poor need more than just *things*. She says that most of all the poor need to know that someone loves them.

Prince Charles of England (left) tours a children's
home run by Mother Teresa.

"It is not what we do," she says,
"but the love we put into what we
do."

So she and her workers go to
the poor with food and medicine
— and love. To those poor people,
they must look like angels in the
slums.

Professor John Sanness (above) hands Mother Teresa her
Nobel Peace Prize in a ceremony held in Oslo, Norway.

King Olav V of Sweden (above) congratulates
Mother Teresa. Everybody smiled when tiny
Mother Teresa met economist John
Kenneth Galbraith (right), who stands over
six feet tall. But Mother Teresa
has proved that you don't have
to be tall or big to change the world.

A Drop in the Ocean

People all over the world respect Mother Teresa for her work. She has won many awards —from India, England, Italy, and the United States. The United Nations made medals with her face on them. And in 1979 the Nobel Peace Prize was given to her.

Mother Teresa uses the award money to help the poor. But she says she can't go to any more ceremonies in her honor. They take too much time away from her work.

Mother Teresa travels around the world helping people. She believes the poor need love as well as food and medicine.

Mother Teresa sees many sad things. But she isn't sad about her work. She believes that God is in all of the poor people she serves — no matter what their religion. For her, serving them is just like serving God.

"The poor are great people," she says.

Once she took some rice to a starving family. The mother of the family gave half of the rice to her neighbor. "They are starving, too," she said.

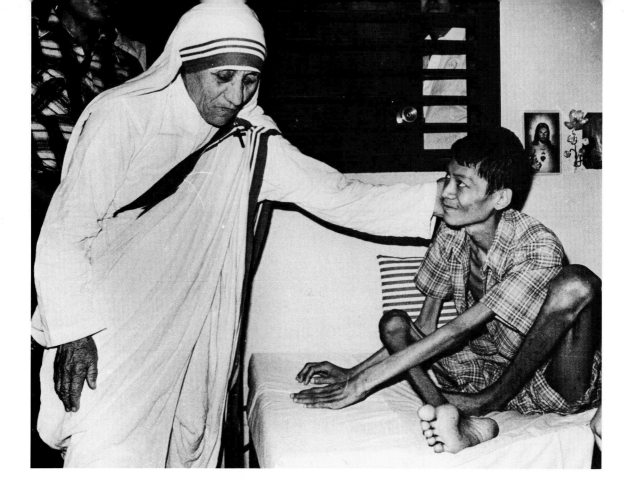

Whether she is greeting a polio victim in the Philippines or
university students in Japan, Mother Teresa is welcomed with affection.

Caring for the poor and
the homeless of all ages,
Mother Teresa is a living example of
what someone who has love,
determination, and courage
can do to change things.

Over the years Mother Teresa has helped many thousands of poor people. Some people say, "To help a few is not enough. It's only a drop in the ocean. There are still millions of poor people left."

To those people Mother Teresa says, "The ocean is made up of drops."

Many years ago, Saint Francis de Sales wrote: "It takes only one good woman to overcome a city."

He could have been writing about Mother Teresa.

MOTHER TERESA

1910	August 27 — Born in Skopje, Yugoslavia, to an Albanian family; named Agnes Gonxha Bojaxhiu
1931	Took temporary religious vows with Sisters of Our Lady of Loreto in India; took the name Teresa for Saint Therese of the Child Jesus
1937	Took final religious vows
1946	Felt called to serve the very poor
1948	Left the Sisters of Loreto, but remained a nun, studied hygiene; moved to slums of Calcutta
1950	Missionaries of Charity approved as an order
1962	Presented with the *Padma Shri* (Lotus Order) by the Indian government
1965	Missionaries of Charity named a Pontifical Congregation by Pope Paul VI
1970	Presented with the Good Samaritan Prize and the Kennedy Foundation award in the United States
1971	Received the Pope John XXIII Peace Prize
1972	Presented with India's Jawaharlal Nehru Award for International Understanding
1973	Presented with the Templeton Prize in London
1975	Presented with the Albert Schweitzer Award in the United States; a United Nations medallion was minted in her honor
1979	Presented with the Balzan Award in Italy and received the Nobel Peace Prize
1989	Had a heart attack and received a pacemaker
1990	Inaugurates a home for children in Romania where an AIDS epidemic strikes hundreds of young
1991	Periodically writes reflections and explanations about missionary work for *L'osservatore Romano*

About the Author

CAROL GREENE has a B.A. in English Literature from Park College, Parkville, Missouri and an M.A. in Musicology from Indiana University, Bloomington. She's worked with international exchange programs, taught music and writing, and edited children's books. She now works as a free-lance writer in St. Louis, Missouri and has had published over 20 books for children and a few for adults. When she isn't writing, Ms. Greene likes to read, travel, sing, and do volunteer work at her church. Her other books for Childrens Press include: *The Super Snoops and the Missing Sleepers, Sandra Day O'Connor—First Woman on the Supreme Court, Rain! Rain!, Please Wind?, Snow Joe,* and *The New True Book of Holidays Around the World.*